BETHLEHEM

BETHLEHEM

A NATIVITY PLAY
BY LAURENCE HOUSMAN
PERFORMED WITH MUSIC
BY JOSEPH MOORAT UNDER
THE STAGE–DIRECTION OF
EDWARD GORDON CRAIG
DECEMBER MCMII

New York

THE MACMILLAN COMPANY
LONDON: MACMILLAN AND CO., LTD.
1902

COPYRIGHT, 1902,

By THE MACMILLAN COMPANY.

———

Set up and electrotyped December, 1902.

Norwood Press
J. S. Cushing & Co. — Berwick & Smith
Norwood Mass. U.S.A.

ACT I

ACT I

Chorus enters and speaks before the curtain

Ye Gentles, that come here to watch our play,

Put, we beseech you, thought of us away!

No standing here have we: in heart we kneel,

With, at our hearts, this prayer, — that ye may feel

How in Love's hands time is a little thing!

And so shall Love to-night your senses bring

Back to the hills of Bethlehem, the fold

Where shepherds watched their sheep, where angels

    told

Of peace, goodwill to men, in Christ new-born,

By whom, from Virgin Birth, our flesh goes worn.

Also, if we may guide you, ye shall see

The manger where in great humility

3

Lieth that Babe, the Maker of us all,

By Mary's side, amid the beasts in stall.

And ye shall see the coming of the Kings,

Led by a star; and Gabriel that brings

Unto St. Joseph in a dream by night

Word of King Herod's fear, and counsels flight.

So, lastly, ye shall see them rise and go,

And the place vacant left. Yet ye shall know

That Love remains, and that Faith sees it so.

So, have ye hope! let Time your trust increase!

Hark, I hear music! Christmas comes; 'tis peace!

Pastoral music: a shepherd's voice is heard

'The world is old, to-night,

   The world is old;

The stars around the fold

Do show their light, do show their light.

And so they did, and so

A thousand years ago,

And so will do, dear love, when you lie cold.'

[*The curtain opens, and discloses a bare field with a scarp of rock to the right: in the background are low hills covered with snow. To the left lies a fold surrounded by high wattles. Under shelter of the rock six shepherds are gathered: overhead, with his feet hanging over the ledge, a boy wrapped in a sheepskin sits to keep watch, and at intervals give the watcher's cry.*

YOUNG SHEPHERD (*sings*)

The world is still, to-night,

The world is still:

The snow on vale and hill

    Like wool lies white, like wool lies white.

And so it was, and so

A thousand years ago,

    And so will be, good lads, when we lack will.

WATCHER

Ay-oh, ay-oh, ay-oh !

1ST SHEPHERD

There be good fairies up in air to-night :

Come ere a frost so mild with stars so bright?

The wind has shut itself in-door again,

And all the air be saft like a'ter rain.

WATCHER

Ay-oh, ay-oh, ay-oh !

2ND SHEPHERD (*rising*)

The sheep be quiet; the dogs have nought to do;

The lambs come kind; there haven't been a ewe

Lost, nor a still one born, this moon, there an't:

A thing I can't remember, nor I can't

Since I've been shepherd: — that's nigh forty year.

3RD SHEPHERD

Well, well!

4TH SHEPHERD

What star be that'n out yonder there?

It's been a-coming on, night a'ter night,

This long time back, but never looked so bright

As 'a do now.

WATCHER

Ay-oh, ay-oh, ay-oh!

4TH SHEPHERD

D'you think stars have a way

Of coming out like, special, when they got summat

   to say?

I've often wondered how it is they are:

You never seem to get no nearer to a star, —

Walk after 'em a mile they still seem just as far.

3RD SHEPHERD

'Tis as God made 'em. Like as they were geese,

Go a'ter 'em, and they turns tail and flees;

Then you go back, and back they come at you!

So as God made 'em's what they got to do.

1ST SHEPHERD

Aye, I don't doubt the stars lays facts to mind.

There's them as say men's names be marked and
    signed, —

Writ in the roof up there, for proof that God's
    behind.

WATCHER

Ay-oh, ay-oh, ay-oh!

5TH SHEPHERD

You think a star knows what it's all about,

A-blazing for?

1ST SHEPHERD

I haven't got a doubt

He does! That star — now don't tell me no more.

You think he don't know what he's shining for!

Look at him jerking and working, and a-winking and

a-blinking : —

Well, — that's him thinking.

3RD SHEPHERD

Well, if he thinks the things God sets him to,

Like we poor men, he's got enough to do!

WATCHER

Ay-oh, ay-oh, ay-oh!

4TH SHEPHERD

There's old blind Abe a-looking! Don't he seem
As if he saw it?

2ND SHEPHERD

Aye! he likes to dream
He's won his sight back, tho' it's been twelve year
    gone.
Abe, what d'you think you've got your eye upon?

ABEL

A good sight! aye, and a sight as you can't see
So well as I. The thought just come to me,
While all of you sat talking by my side,
Like to the word the prophet prophesied; —

And while you talked, the thought o' it kep' me
    dumb : —

Shiloh, thinks I, — will I see Shiloh come?

And all at once these words were in my head, —

What he, — the man whose eyes were open — said

Aforetime, 'I shall see him ; — but not now !'

Says he, 'I shall behold him ; — but not nigh :

Out of Jacob there shall come forth a star,

And a Sceptre in Israel shall be raised high.'

So he bare witness of things seen afar,

And that being told so many years ago,

Yet still to come, do surely seem to show

How we be likelier to behold that star

Than he who only spoke o' it from afar.

And in that day, 'tis told, the dumb shall talk,

The old shall leap, and the lame man shall walk,

And the blind man recover back his sight !

3RD SHEPHERD

Well, well, it may be so! God will do right.

1ST SHEPHERD

May we be there to see when that day shows:
What it can do for such as we — God knows!

WATCHER

Ay-oh! . . .

> [*Breaks off suddenly, leaps down from the rock,
> and seizing* 1ST SHEPHERD, *points terror-
> stricken. A sound of wind is heard.*

1ST SHEPHERD

Why! who be yon fine gentleman in white
Stepping across the sheepfolds to the right?

4TH SHEPHERD

How comes it that his face be lit so bright?

3RD SHEPHERD

The blood pricks in my thumbs;
'Tis like a ghost he comes!

[*They huddle fearfully under the rock, crossing
themselves.*

Enter GABRIEL (*He makes the sign of the cross*)

GABRIEL

Let nothing you annoy!
Behold, I bring

Good tidings of great joy:

To you a King

This day is born, to you and all mankind.

Even Christ the Lord, to earthly state resigned.

3RD SHEPHERD

Oh Lord, oh Lord! was ever the like heard tell.

ABEL

Hold ye your peace, neighbours! he speaks us well.

GABRIEL

And of that same

Let this be for a sign.

In Bethlehem

Cradled amid the kine,
A Babe in swaddling bands ye there shall find.

4TH SHEPHERD

Have you no fear? oh, Abel, but you're blind!

ABEL

Peace, and give ear! New light shines in my
mind.

GABRIEL

And as a shepherd he shall feed
    His flocks, and in his arms shall bear
    The lambs, and like a father fair
The ewes with young shall lead.

Angels *appear*

Angels

SEMI-CHORUS   SEMI-CHORUS

Glory to God   In the Highest!

Who unto man   Now comes nighest,

Peace be to earth!   Goodwill to all!

Christ the new birth   Redeems man's fall.

Gabriel

Ye holy and humble men of fearful heart,

Be not afraid with these to take your part.

To-night God gives you sight; then be not blind.

Behold with us the high celestial mind.

Ye also with one voice must here rejoice!

C

1st Shepherd

We be poor mortals !   Here's all Heaven in sight !

Gabriel

The Heavens themselves are joined with earth
    to-night.
Fear not, but rise, Mercy and Truth are met ;
And Righteousness on Peace her seal hath set.
        Stand and be strong,
            Ye, too, shall share our song !

Semi-Chorus

Glory to God ; on earth, peace, goodwill !
He smites with His rod, and the waters are still ;
He maketh it bud for the evil and good,
He lifts the low valley and bends the high hill.

Thou Christ art the Rod, and Thy reign shall be
  peace !

At the power of Thy nod, all warfare shall cease.

The desert shall blossom and be as the rose,

When the healing of nations from Bethlehem flows.

CHORUS AND SEMI-CHORUS

Glory to God	In the Highest !
Who unto man	Now comes nighest,
Peace be to earth !	Goodwill to all !
Christ the new birth	Redeems man's fall.

[*The* ANGELS *disappear.*

4TH SHEPHERD

Sir, have we dreamed this?

GABRIEL

Let your own hearts tell!
Do dreams bequeath such joy? Your bosoms swell,
Your faces glow, your eyes are full of cheer!
Why are they so? Lately you had great fear,
And stood as huddled flocks before a storm;
Have dreams then made you warm?

4TH SHEPHERD

Oh, Sir, 'tis true.
Yet scarcely do I know what next to do.

2ND SHEPHERD

You come wi' me, lad! come along o' me!
We'll all be off to Bethlehem, and see

What they be doing there! Lord, Lord, I doubt

Whether I'll know to find me way about

With such high things a-happening!

                                   Sir, you see

There ain't much show about the likes o' we,

But what I say's — if this be true — well, well,

'Tis the best news that ever I heard tell!

1st Shepherd

And the best fortune any on us has had!

Lord, though, but don't it make an old heart glad!

Christ born? You say it is so, Sir? So be it!

Thank God that we should be alive to see it!

Abel

Be He at Bethlehem?

GABRIEL

Aye, there go ye!
While ye so fare, your folds shall guarded be;
Round them even now stand those ye do not see.
Go ye in peace!

SHEPHERDS

We thank you kindly, Sir.

SHEPHERDS (*sing*)

Now we will go, now we will go,
　The way we know to Bethlehem;
That they may show, and we may know,
　'Tis even so as you proclaim.

And we will take the bread we bake,
　The wine we make as gifts to them,

And milk and cheese, and on our knees
Will offer these at Bethlehem.

And He shall know we love Him so,
But cannot show a better way
Of service dear, and loving cheer,
Than we do here on Christmas Day.

[*Exeunt several of the* SHEPHERDS.

4TH SHEPHERD

Sir, do you think that I might make so bold
As offer Him a young lamb from the fold?
'Twas the first dropped this lambing time; maybe
He'll take it kindly from the likes o' we,
We being simple shepherds.

GABRIEL

Simple? Yes!

Would God, all minds had this same simpleness!
Take Him what gifts ye will! To-night on earth
All's peace to greet Christ's birth.

> [*He makes the sign of the cross on them, and
> turns away.*

5TH SHEPHERD

Noticed you that?
He made the shepherd's sign: 'a did it pat!

SHEPHERDS (*without*)

Come on, lads, come!

4TH SHEPHERD

Good-night, Sir.

GABRIEL
                              Peace befall
You and your ways! Good-night, friend; good-
night, all.   [*Exeunt* SHEPHERDS.

SHEPHERDS (*in the distance singing*)

And we will go, and we will go,
    The way we know to Bethlehem;
That Love may show, and we may know,
    'Tis even so as you proclaim.

[*With the song of the shepherds blends faintly the
    singing of angels and swells till the song of
    the* KINGS *is heard.* GABRIEL *has covered
    himself with a shepherd's cloak and stands
    leaning on a shepherd's crook by the rock
    overlooking the fold. A light begins steadily
    to increase and flood the stage. Enter*

presently the ANGEL OF THE STAR. *As he crosses the stage, bearing the* STAR *in his hands,* GABRIEL *kneels down in reverence. The* ANGEL OF THE STAR *departs by the road to Bethlehem.*

Enter the KINGS (*they advance singing*)

1ST KING

Hear me, O King of Kings,
And give me my desire !

2ND KING

Hive me beneath Thy wings,
And guide my feet with fire !

3RD KING

Unto that Holy Mount,
    Where forth from Thee goes Light.

ALL

Whence springs a Living Fount
    To wash the whole world white.

[*The* KINGS *descend and advance to the front of
the stage. During what follows their trains
pass in silence upon the way to Bethlehem,
led by the* STAR *whose light is still seen
diminishing.*

GABRIEL

Peace be with you, and hail!

Where go ye this fair night,

Travellers, and what seek ye?

1ST KING

We seek from the hill the vale,

And from the vale the hill.

2ND KING

From the ends of the morning, rest;

And from the East the West.

3RD KING

In the darkness we seek fire,

And out of dreams the heart's desire!

And, if to-day we fail,
To-morrow we seek it still.

GABRIEL

Are ye not weary, seeking so?
Are ye not laden with care?

1ST KING

We are not weary. If our feet be slow,
'Tis with the burden of the Love we bear.
It is our longing for the Light we seek
Which makes us weak.

GABRIEL

What is the longing of each one?

3RD KING

Melchior, wilt thou first speak?

2ND KING

Too slow my footsteps move

For the goal I seek to prove.

My body is a waste,

Through which my soul doth haste,

Famished until it taste

Its nameless new desire!

A flame my spirit owns,

Ashes are all my bones,

Love lights in me such fire!

I thirst! my throat is dried!

I ask;—am still denied!

Cry to be satisfied:

Yet only as Love will.

Now, if He come not first,

Not death, but ease were worst ; —

Let me die, thirsting still !

GABRIEL

And you?

3RD KING

I have such Love !

Beauty, I know not of

Hath laid on me the vision of its Light.

When that Light shines, earth's ends

Therein shall all be friends :

They shall not hurt nor kill, but on the height

Named Holy shall be peace.

Then shall all warfare cease,

And every king his crown

Shall at the cradle of a new-born Babe lay down.

GABRIEL

And thou, that standest last,

Say what desire thou hast?

1ST KING

For Earth's waiting to be done;

For God to send His Son,

Godhead and man made one!

That creation, wrought afresh,

May be finished and made whole;

That the Word may become Flesh,

And earth receive her soul!

Pray we for this,

Seeing well how good it is.

GABRIEL

Behold, this night shall bring you to your bliss.

3RD KING

Whence comes thy knowledge to make hope so
near?

GABRIEL

Oh, let your ears be opened till they hear!

Open your eyes, and mark with fearless sight

The throng of thanksgiving which fills this night:

Nor walks on heaven alone, but earth as well!

Sound in sweet tone, celestial choirs, and tell!

D

Angels (*appearing*)

Glory to God	In the Highest!
Who unto man	Now comes nighest!
Peace be to earth!	Goodwill to all!
Christ the new birth	Redeems man's fall!

1st King

Oh, ye blest sounds, be as the air we breathe!

2nd King

Oh, fair things seen, your light to us bequeath.

3rd King

And if there be an ending to our quest,

Show, now, where lies our rest!

GABRIEL

Oh, Kings, your quest is ended now; earth joins

To greet her Lord, in Heaven's exultant strains.

Righteousness is the girdle of His loins,

And faithfulness the girdle of His reins.

The Spirit of God shall rest on Him, of might,

Of wisdom, and of counsel, and of fear:

He shall not judge according unto sight,

Neither reprove by the hearing of His ear:

But by His righteousness shall He do right,

And with His equity the meek repay,

Out of His mouth a rod the earth shall smite;

And by His breath the wicked He shall slay.

The wolf shall make his dwelling in the fold,

The leopard and the kid together play,

The young lion with the fatling: and behold

A Little Child shall lead them in the way!

Then like the ox the lion shall eat straw,

The calf and the young bear be in one pen;

The suckling from his hole the asp shall draw,

And the weaned child play by the adder's den.

They shall not hurt in all my Holy Hill

Nor shall there any more destruction be:

The knowledge of the Lord the earth shall fill,

Even as the water covereth the sea.

And He shall raise His people from their sin.

This is the way of Life: walk ye therein!

[*A vision of a* YOUNG CHILD *appears.*

1st KING

Where shall we find Him? when throw off our
    load?

GABRIEL

In Bethlehem Peace makes His fair abode.

Yonder His star still lights you to your road.

[*The* KINGS *depart.* GABRIEL *makes the sign
of blessing, and is taken up into Heaven.*

ACT II

ACT II

[*The inn-stable at Bethlehem. An open court, sur-*
rounded on three sides by cattle-sheds with thatched
roofs. In the centre stands a 'cradle' for fodder,
above which hangs a canopy rudely constructed of
a cloak thrown over a traveller's staff thrust into
the eaves of the thatch, from which also hangs a
small lantern. Above the roof shows a clear
starlit sky. At the back of the stable to the right
is a door opening to the street: to the left a cave
in a wall of rock, shut off by a large grille, behind
which the beasts are stalled. MARY *reclines in the*
'cradle,' with the child concealed beneath her robe.
JOSEPH *sits near by to the left. His shoes lie near*

him, together with lantern, water-skins, and saddle
packs.   He bends over a scroll of parchment.
Without voices are heard singing.

'Noel, Noel, Noel,'
 Sang the church bell;
'God's in His Heaven,
 This know well!'

'Noel, Noel, Noel,'
 Ding, dong-bell,
'God from High Heaven
 Comes on earth to dwell.'

'Noel, Noel, Noel,'
 Bells ring on earth,
'Come and know well
 This bright Birth!'

JOSEPH (*rising and advancing to the cradle*)

Sleepest thou, Mary?

MARY

                   I sleep not, I pray!

Behold, on me my Lord His Head doth lay.

Look how in sleep He takes a mortal's rest :

See where His Hand is laid upon my breast !

JOSEPH

Mary, I dread to see !

MARY

              Nay, come more near ;

But wake Him not !

JOSEPH

Alas! I have such fear.

MARY

I, too : my soul is glad through very dread

While in this chamber God doth make His bed :

For now our eyes behold the glorious Birth

Which shall uplift again low-fallen earth.

Here, where He rests, amid these hollowed rocks,

I hear the world's heart move in joyful shocks,

The pulsing of her rivers and her springs :

I feel the air beat with the throb of wings :

And farther up, amid the heavenly maze,

The stars and planets with adoring gaze

Look down and say, ' O maid with favour stored

How com'st thou to be Mother of our Lord?'

What can I answer, I? Let Gabriel

Speak to those heavenly questioners, and tell

How by the Holy Ghost this came to be;

How power from the Highest o'ershadowed me,

Till in my heart God came Himself to lie,

Perfect fulfilment of all prophecy.

Naught may I know save this: His handmaid I.

VOICES

'Ave Maria, gratia plena, Dominus tecum!
benedicta tu in mulieribus, et benedictus fructus
ventris tui, Jesus.'

*[A knocking is heard, and a sound of pastoral
music. JOSEPH, crossing before the crib,
makes a reverence. He goes to the door.*

JOSEPH

Who knocks ?

SHEPHERD (*without*)

　　　A friend: we be all friendly men:
We be the shepherds.

JOSEPH

　　　Come in, shepherds, then:
Here's welcome waiting you !　Behold and bless
The peace within your gates, the plenteousness !

The SHEPHERDS *enter.　As they come within sight*
*　　　of the crib they draw their hats over their*
*　　　faces and down to their breasts.　They dip*

their fingers in a water-stoup, cross themselves, and kneel. MARY *makes the sign of the cross to them in greeting.*

1ST SHEPHERD

Mother of God, welcome to Bethlehem.

MARY

Shepherds of Israel, welcome to Christ's Birth.

OMNES

Hail Mary, full of grace, the Lord is with thee ! Blessed art thou among women, and blessed is the fruit of thy womb — Jesus. Holy Mary, Mother of God, pray for us sinners now, and in the hour of our death. Amen.

MARY

Behold the handmaid of the Lord!

So as His Word hath His Way been;

Now Earth to Heaven doth room afford;

The Godhead veiled in flesh is seen.

Come and adore, in form of man,

The Word that was ere worlds began.

[*She raises herself, and sits with her mantle
still covering the Holy Child.*

OMNES

Mother Mary, hail!

And of thy Grace,

Lift away the veil

That hides God's face!

Here God lies

For a short space.

Mary, Mother wise,

Show us God's face!

Mary, all the lands,

Mary, all the seas,

Gather in thy hands

To thy dear knees!

Mary, maiden white,

Mother pure within,

Show to mortal sight

Love that cures sin!

1st Shepherd

Mother Mary, may we see God?

E

MARY

Stand near in faith, behold,

   Be comforted by Him!

Here, shepherds, is your fold.

ABEL

Lady, I cannot see : mine eyes are dim.

MARY

Come near, in faith : come near!

   Thou shalt win sight.

Doubt not : have thou no fear!

ABEL

Lady, mine eyes be healed and full of light!

MARY

Even so, even so,

Let Earth perceive and know!

[JOSEPH *aiding*, MARY *lifts her mantle, and
reveals* CHRIST *to them. They all kneel and
bow themselves.*

1ST SHEPHERD

Son of God, shine on us!

2ND SHEPHERD

Lamb of God, look on us!

3RD SHEPHERD

Shepherd of men, set Thy sign on us!

4TH SHEPHERD

And lay Thy yoke on us !

5TH SHEPHERD

And we will be thankful.

[MARY *again covers the Child.*

1ST SHEPHERD

Queen, Mother, pardon me who make so bold
To speak; but hearts grown full be hard to hold.
To-night, as Heaven hath willed, have come thy way
Poor folk with meagre speech yet much to say.
So, if word lack, let thine own wisdom fill:
And — give me countenance, — I'll not speak ill.
Dear Mother, pray for us ! Foolish we be,
Untaught and rude : but what we see we see,

And what we hear we hear; to what's above

Our heads we bow: and what we love we love!

And, loving thee since our first entrance in,

Do thereby more love God, and more hate sin;

And of all lips would have thy lips to pray

Pardon for us and peace to seek His way.

  Fair Mother, we have old men here among,

As thou may'st see; and thou, we see, art young:

Yet the name 'Mother' runneth to the tongue

That seeks a name for thee. May we not all

Thee as our Lady and our Mother call,

For thy Son's sake?

MARY

Amen. So, shepherds, do!

Call as love bids you, and I'll answer you.

  [*The* SHEPHERDS *now advance and present their*
    offerings.

1ST SHEPHERD

Mother, I have laid bread here at thy feet.

For thy Son's sake, I pray thee take and eat!

2ND SHEPHERD

Mother, I bring thee milk.

3RD SHEPHERD

I bring thee cheese.

4TH SHEPHERD

I have brought nuts. Strengthen His teeth on
    these,

When they begin to pair.

5TH SHEPHERD

Also here's wine,

Good for a festal, or when frost bites fine.

Also my cloak is thine.

6TH SHEPHERD

Dear Mother, for God's sake,

Wilt thou, I prithee, take

This firstling from the fold?

It is so beautiful,

And thereto hath warm wool

To ward one from the cold.

Take it, then, to thy lap

Beside thy Son:

It may keep warm, mayhap,

The Blessed One.

MARY

It shall keep warm my heart, shepherd, to thee.

7TH SHEPHERD

Mother, my empty hands do me a wrong:
No gift have I, but in my lips a song
    Such as we shepherds sing.

MARY

                        Such songs are best.
To-night your lips shall lull the Shepherd's King
    To rest.

7TH SHEPHERD

    The world is old to-night (*sings*),
        The world is old:

The stars around the fold

Do show their light.

And so they did, and so,

A thousand years ago.

And so will do, dear Love, when you lie cold.

(*Speaks.*) Nay, nay, but I can sing no more thereof;

I had forgot the sadness of the end!

MARY

Thou hast but prophesied how men shall scoff

Even at Love, my friend.

[Knocking is heard.

JOSEPH

Ho, there without! Who knocks? Come ye in

peace?

KINGS (*without*)

Kings, seeking it, we come!

JOSEPH

Here enter, and find ease!

The KINGS *enter, and advance kneeling three times.*

1ST KING

Blessed be God!

OMNES

Blessed be God!

2ND KING

Blessed be His Holy Name!

OMNES

Blessed be His Holy Name!

3RD KING

Blessed be Jesus Christ, true God and true Man!

OMNES

Blessed be Jesus Christ, true God and true Man!

1ST KING

Oh, finished quest!

Oh, rest!

2ND KING

Oh, Fount, that first

Of all hath satisfied my thirst!

3RD KING

Oh, Light,

That brings me sight!

[*The* KINGS *approach in turn, and kneel before
the cradle.*

1ST KING

Thou Birth Divine,

Behold,

The earthly sign

Of power and kingship, gold,

Here in my hands I hold,

And offer, to be Thine.

2ND KING

This frankincense

Let be

A symbol whence

All men may learn to see

How veiled a mystery

Defeats man's sense where Godhead deigns to be.

3RD KING

Oh, Comforter of souls,

    I bring thee myrrh.

When grief my heart controls

And darkness round me rolls,

    Sweet Saviour, be Thou near!

THE THREE KINGS

Thanksgiving, Praise, and Prayer,

    Three offerings meet,

We lay in equal share

    Before Christ's feet.

MARY

Your welcome gifts,

Proffered in love, from Earth to Heaven He lifts.

THE KINGS

Now see we Love on Earth His throne!

All we have known,

Or hoped to gain,

Was this alone —

That He might reign.

OMNES

That He might reign!

Oh, welcome Birth! let all adore

The Christ made Man for evermore.

The Shepherds

'Tis Christmas morn,

    Come ye, and bow the knee!

    Lo, here we see

The perfect Man is born.

Chorus

(*In alternate parts*, Kings *and* Shepherds)

    For this fair Birth

        (Which now we see)

    Shows forth God's worth

        (Then sing we merrily!)

    And makes glad earth.

    And brings man mirth

        (So sing we merrily this fair Birth!)

The Kings

'Tis Christmas Day,

    Oh pray, — put off your sins!

    This day begins

For man the perfect way.

Chorus (*as before*)

For this fair Birth, etc.

[*During this song the attendants of the* Kings
    *creep softly in and kneel in an outer ring
    under shadow of the sheds.*

Omnes

Mother Mary, give us thy Son's Blessing.

                [*All kneel.*

(*They sing*) Mary, Gate of Day,

       Lend thine intercession !

Holy Mother May,

       Pray for my transgression !

Ere He yet touched Earth,

       He did first touch thee ;

Through thy perfect worth

       God reached down for me.

MARY. [*Rises and stands in the cradle under shadow of the canopy, displaying the child in her breast, still partly covered by her veil.* JOSEPH *and one of the* SHEPHERDS *lift and draw back the ends of her long robe.*

    The word expressed

       In Flesh hath come ;

F

Against my breast

The Voice lies dumb,

That shall be of all prophecies the sum.

Oh, Thou dread Voice

Of Heaven's decree,

Who madest choice

To dwell with me,

Now through my lips, this once, let utterance be !

My Peace I leave,

My Peace I give :

All that receive

The same shall live ;

And tribute hearts win joy retributive.

The Cup I bless,

The Bread I break,

Is Righteousness !

Draw near and take !

Eat, drink, and hold remembrance for Love's sake !

The peace of Peace,

Outpassing sense,

Give your minds ease

When ye go hence.

Love, peace, and pardon be your recompense.

Omnes

Hail, Mary, full of grace, the Lord is with thee ! Blessed art thou among women, and blessed is the fruit of thy womb — Jesus. Holy Mary, Mother of God, pray for us sinners now, and in the hour of our death. Amen.

Mary

Kings from far countries have ye come to see A King whose reign shall make all kingdoms free.

Low at His feet your crowns ye cast to ground;

From this day forward ye shall go more crowned;

For, named hereafter, ye shall be named wise,

Seeing that in Heaven ye watched Christ's star arise.

Great kings ye came : but much more great ye go,

Who to His state have bowed yourselves so low.

And you, dear Shepherds, to your settled folds

Return, and father your sweet flocks to rest!

Though Heavenly signs depart, Heaven's purpose
   holds

Where Earth's Redemption slumbers at my breast.

Look where He lies! Kiss ye His feet, and go!

Your Shepherd He : whose sheep are ye, I know.

[*Now, as she speaks, one by one they advance
   and do homage, and return to their places.*

When mothers teach to babes their mother-tongue,

   This tale shall first be told —

How to His birth ye came in days of old,

While starlight led and seraph-voices sung.

So, in that story, shall your names stay young.

Farewell; give thanks for this! Ye to Christ's
fold

Are come. Take all the bliss that hearts on
earth may hold!

[*All kneel in silence. The starlight fades and
the stage darkens: only the light of the
lantern remains. One by one* SHEPHERDS
and KINGS *rise, make a reverence toward
the crib, cross themselves, and depart.*
JOSEPH *closes the door after them. He lets
down the curtains of the canopy over the
sleeping Mother and Child, lays by the
offerings of the* SHEPHERDS *and* KINGS,
and sinks down wearily to rest. In the

surrounding darkness appear the faces of angels watching. They disappear after GABRIEL *has spoken to* JOSEPH. *Outside the* SHEPHERDS *and* KINGS *are heard singing till their voices die away in the distance.*

SHEPHERDS AND KINGS (*without*)

I heard on Christmas night
    The loud bells ringing:
'New Life and Light
    Christ comes bringing!'

Chorus

Oh, that is true, is true,
    And better could not be!
So God bless you!
    And God bless me!

I heard on Christmas night
    The glad news pealing:
'Christ to human sight
    Now gives healing!'

    Oh, that is true, is true,
        And better could not be!
    So God bless you!
        And God bless me!

I heard on Christmas night
    The High Heavens telling:
'Christ who left His height,
    On earth finds dwelling!'

    Oh, that is true, is true,
        And better could not be!
    So God bless you!
        And God bless me!

From Mary, Queen of Might,

　　Comes down sweet saying:

'I hear, on Christmas night,

　　All poor hearts praying!'

Oh, that is true, is true,

　　And better could not be!

So God bless you!

　　And God bless me!

Enter GABRIEL

GABRIEL

Servant of God, sleep not, awake!

　　Saddle the ass ere dawn of day;

The Mother, and the young Child take

　　Whom Herod seeketh now to slay.

Get thee hence ere the wakening bird

Hath sung: to Egypt win thy way:

There, till I come and bring thee word,

Shalt thou in hiding stay.

As thou hast heard, make haste, obey!

[*Exit.* JOSEPH *lies heavy with sleep: he stirs
slowly and, with great pain, rising, goes and
kneels where the angel has stood. Then he
goes to the stable and makes ready, opening
doors beyond which lead on to the street;
then returning he rouses* MARY *from sleep.*

JOSEPH

Mary, arise; hence must we go

Even before the dawn of day.

MARY

It is God's will?

JOSEPH

'Tis even so :

His angel's word.

MARY

Which we obey.

[*They go out to the stable, whence presently the sound of hoofs is heard as they pass forth.*

VOICES OF CAROL-SINGERS (*without*)

God rest you, merry gentlemen,
    Let nothing you dismay !
Because that Jesus Christ our Lord
    Is born on Christmas Day !

[*Bells are heard, and dawn begins to show. A* STABLEMAN *stumbles in heavy with sleep and carrying a lantern. He looks round surprised to find the place empty. Then on the ground he discovers three gold coins lying. He kneels before the empty crib.*

[CURTAIN]

Enter CHORUS

CHORUS

O maid and Holy Child, where have ye gone?
Lost are the voices: sets the Star that shone:
Back to their folds have gone the shepherd-band:
Each king is now returned to his own land.
Love is gone forth into the world, to win
Saints to their rest, and sinners back from sin.

Gentles, O ye that here have watched our play,

Tell me, I pray you, did He pass *your* way?

Say, have ye Him, safe, each one in his breast?

Oh, hold Him well! So shall we all have rest.

The Grace of Jesus Christ, who is our Lord,

The Love of God, the Holy Ghost's accord,

Be with us all! And Heaven be our reward!

Amen.

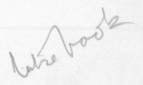

THE HOLY LAND

Pictured in Color

By JOHN FULLEYLOVE, R.I.

Described by the Rev. JOHN KELMAN, M.A. Containing up-
wards of 70 full-page illustrations reproduced in the colors of
the original paintings.

Cloth   8vo $6.00 net

The book is in three parts, of which the first is geographical,
and the second historical. These, however, are in no sense
scientific studies of the geography or the history of Palestine ;
they are only the record of such impressions of these as any
inexpert but open-eyed traveller to-day may receive, and they
lead up to the third part, whose subject is "The Spirit of Syria."

THE LIFE OF CHRIST AS REPRE-
SENTED IN ART

By FREDERIC W. FARRAR, D.D., F.R.S.

Late Fellow of Trinity College, Cambridge; Archdeacon and
Canon of Westminster; Chaplain in Ordinary to the Queen
and to the House of Commons. With numerous illustrations
and frontispiece. *New and cheaper edition.*

8vo   Cloth   Gilt Top $3.50

"The life of Christ, as told by the chief artists of all time in
their most striking works, is here most effectively arranged with
a luminous and edifying commentary text by a writer thoroughly
prepared for his task. . . . It is a book delightful to read.
The illustrations cover a large field of the most important art-
activity of mediæval and modern times." — *The Independent.*

THE MACMILLAN COMPANY
66 FIFTH AVENUE, NEW YORK